DISCOVER SERIES
AFRICA

SPANISH
Bilingual
EDITION

Elando Común

Common Eland

Cobra Egipcia

Egyptian Cobra

Elefante

Elephant

Cabra

Female Goat

Flamingo

Flamingo

Antílope Orix

Gemsbok Antelope

Serpiente Picuda Enana

Dwarf Beaked Snake

Jirafa Madre y el Bebé

Giraffe Mother and Baby

Jirafas

Giraffes

Erizo

Hedgehog

Hipopótamo

Hippopotamus

Hiena

Hyena

Kudu

Kudu

Lechwes

Lechwe

Lémur

Lemur

Familia del León

Lion Family

Avestruz

Ostrich

Rinoceronte con el Becerro

Rhino with Calf

Rinoceronte

Rhinoceros

Rana de Arena

Sand Frog

Antílope

Waterbuck

Toro Watusi

Watusi Bull

Rinoceronte Blanco

White Rhino

Cebra

Zebra

Make Sure to Check Out the Other Discover Series Books from Xist Publishing:

DISCOVER SERIES
OCEAN Animals

DISCOVER SERIES
PUPPIES

DISCOVER SERIES
HORSES

DISCOVER SERIES
FOSSILS

DISCOVER SERIES
BUGS

DISCOVER SERIES
BABY THINGS

DISCOVER SERIES
TOOLS

DISCOVER SERIES
MILITARY Book 1

DISCOVER SERIES
TRANSPORTATION

DISCOVER SERIES
FIREFIGHTER

Published in the United States by Xist Publishing
www.xistpublishing.com

© 2017 First Bilingual Edition by Xist Publishing
Spanish Translation by Victor Santana

Paperback ISBN: 978-1-53240-222-7 Hardcover ISBN: 978-1-53243-916-2 EISBN 978-1-53240-127-5

xist Publishing